what do

Levers

do?

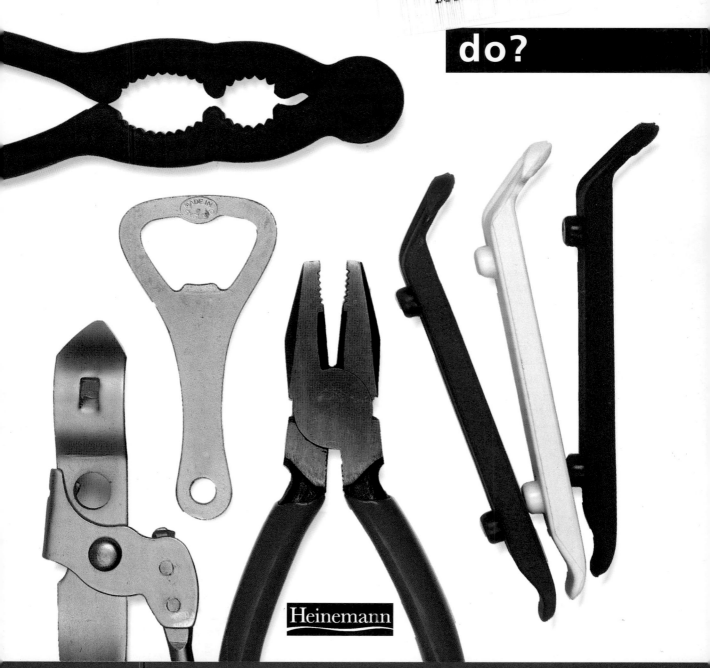

Heinemann

David Glover

First published in Great Britain by Heinemann Library
Halley Court, Jordan Hill, Oxford OX2 8EJ
a division of Reed Educational & Professional Publishing Ltd.

MELBOURNE AUCKLAND
FLORENCE PRAGUE MADRID ATHENS
SINGAPORE TOKYO SÃO PAULO
CHICAGO PORTSMOUTH NH MEXICO
IBADAN GABORONE JOHANNESBURG
KAMPALA NAIROBI

Designed by Celia Floyd and Sharon Rudd
Illustrated by Barry Atkinson (p15), Douglas Hall (pp18, 19), Tony Kenyon (pp5, 9), Ray Straw (p12)
Printed in Hong Kong / China

00 99
10 9 8 7 6 5 4 3

ISBN 0 431 06269 2
This title is also available in a hardback library edition (ISBN 0 431 06268 4).

British Library Cataloguing in Publication Data
Glover, David
   What do levers do?
   1. Levers – Juvenile literature
   I. Title II. Levers
   621.8 ' 2

Acknowledgements
The Publishers would like to thank the following for permission to reproduce photographs:
Trevor Clifford pp4, 6, 7, 8, 9, 10, 11, 12, 14, 15, 21, 23; Collections/Keith Pritchard p16;
Spectrum Colour Library p18; Tony Stone Images p17; Zefa pp13, 22.
Cover photograph by Trevor Clifford.
Commissioned photography arranged by Hilary Fletcher.
Special thanks to Jack, Bejal, Barbara, Alan, Bobby and Rose who appear in the photographs.

Thanks to David Byrne for his comments on the initial draft.

The Publishers would like to thank Toys R Us Ltd The Worlds Biggest Toy Megastore, NES Arnold Ltd, Do It All Ltd and Halfords for the kind loan of equipment and material used in this book.

Every effort has been made to contact copyright holders of any material reproduced in this book. Any omissions will be rectified in subsequent printings if notice is given to the Publisher.

Contents

What are levers? 4

Openers 6

Barrows 8

Tools 10

Crackers and cutters 12

Balances 14

Bridges 16

Rods and oars 18

Brakes 20

Signals 22

Glossary 24

Index 24

What are levers?

A lever is a rod or bar that makes things move. A see-saw is a lever. It has a **pivot** in the middle where it turns. If you push down on one end of a see-saw, the other end goes up.

pivot

A light person can balance a heavy person on a see-saw. The heavier person must sit nearer to the pivot.

This plank is a lever. It pivots at one end. You can use a lever to lift a heavy **load** with a small **effort**, if the load is near the pivot.

effort

lever

load

pivot

Levers do many different jobs inside machines. They change pushes into pulls and they balance weights. Levers also move big loads with small efforts.

Openers

load

pivot

effort

Have you ever opened a tin with the handle of a spoon? The lid fits too tightly to open with your fingers. But when you use the spoon to open the tin, the lid comes off easily.

The spoon handle is the lever. Your hand makes the **effort**. The stiff lid is the **load**. The place where the handle rests on the edge of the tin is the **pivot**.

Magnify your strength!

Levers can *magnify* your strength. They increase the effect of your strength. With a lever you can push or pull much harder than you can with your bare hands. This is why levers are so useful.

A bottle opener is a lever too. It pivots on the bottle top. Your effort as you lift the end of the opener levers the bottle top off.

Barrows

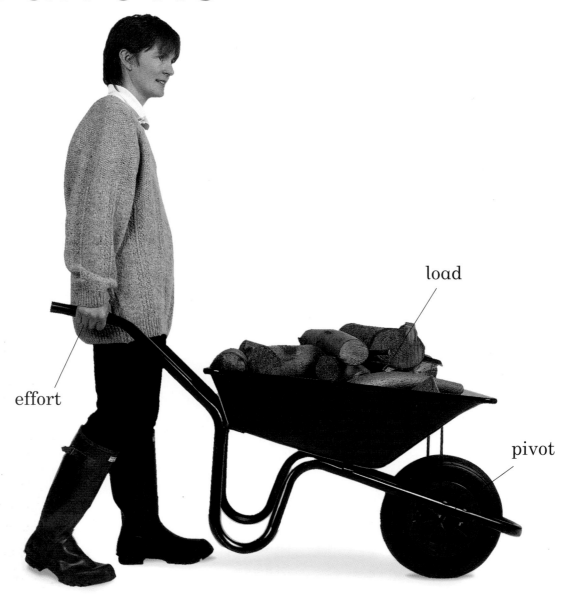

load

effort

pivot

A barrow works as a lever to lift heavy **loads**. A gardener's wheelbarrow **pivots** around the wheel. The gardener's **effort** on the handles is farther away from the pivot than the load. The gardener can lift more in a barrow than in her bare arms.

This porter's barrow has long handles. It levers heavy cases off the ground. When the cases rest over the wheels, the porter can balance them with a small effort.

Moving the world!

In ancient Greece, the scientist Archimedes knew that levers could *magnify* strength. He said: 'Give me a long enough lever and I will move the world!'

Tools

You are not strong enough to pull out a nail with your fingers. But you can lever it out with a **claw hammer**. When you pull on the handle the hammer **pivots** on its head. The claws grip the nail and drag it out of the wood.

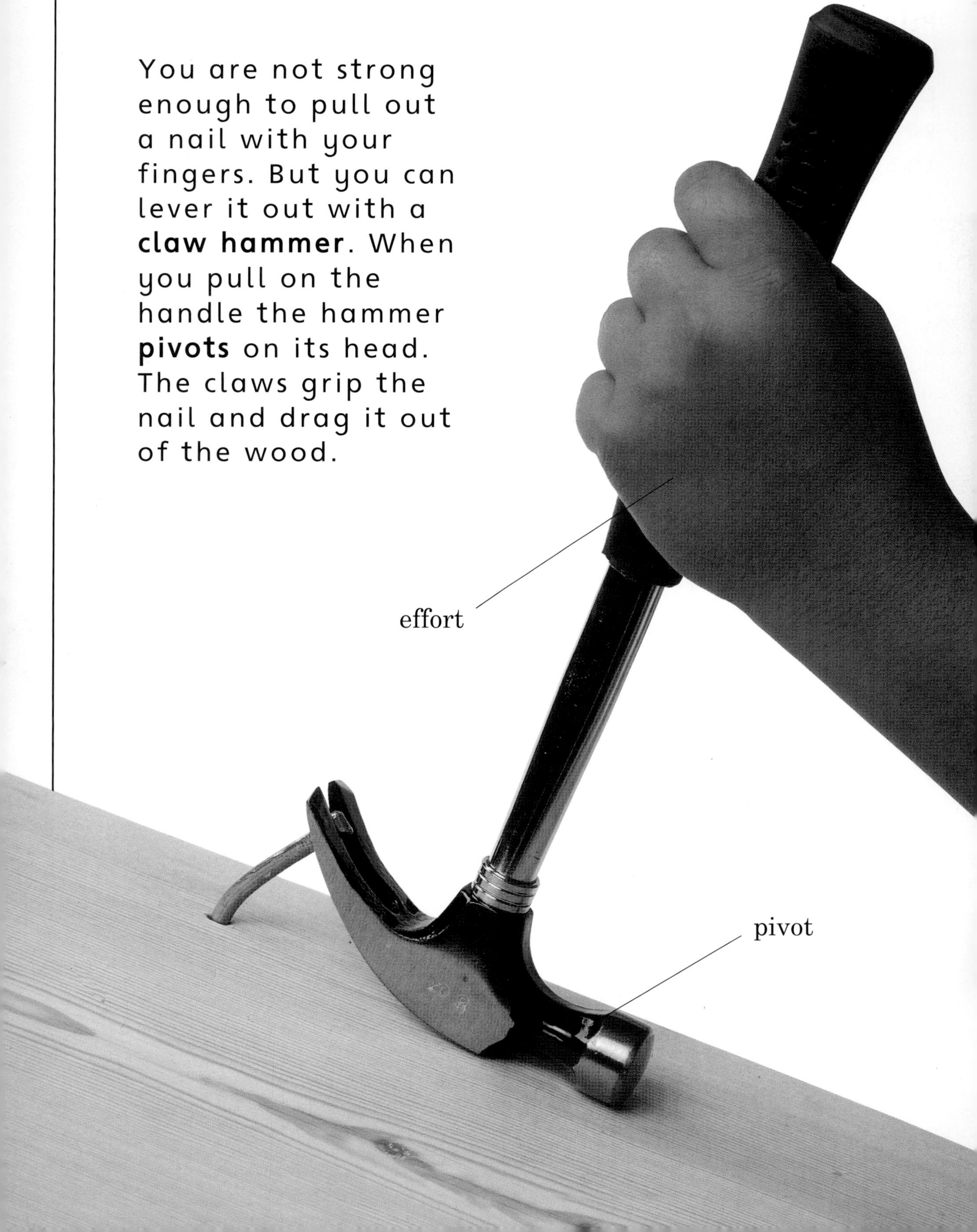

effort

pivot

Pliers are a pair of levers. The jaws are close to the pivot. Pliers can grip with very great force because they have long handles.

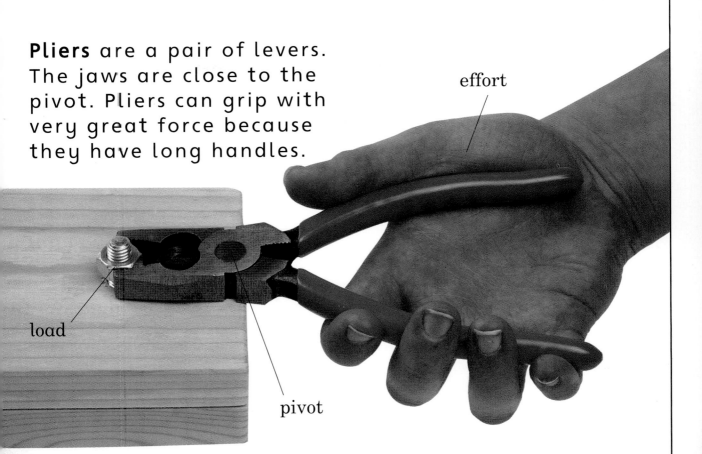

effort

load

pivot

Jaw power!

Your jaws are a pair of levers. They work like pliers. Your back teeth are closer to the hinge of your jaws than your front teeth, so they can bite harder. That is why it is easier to crunch a carrot with your back teeth.

Crackers and cutters

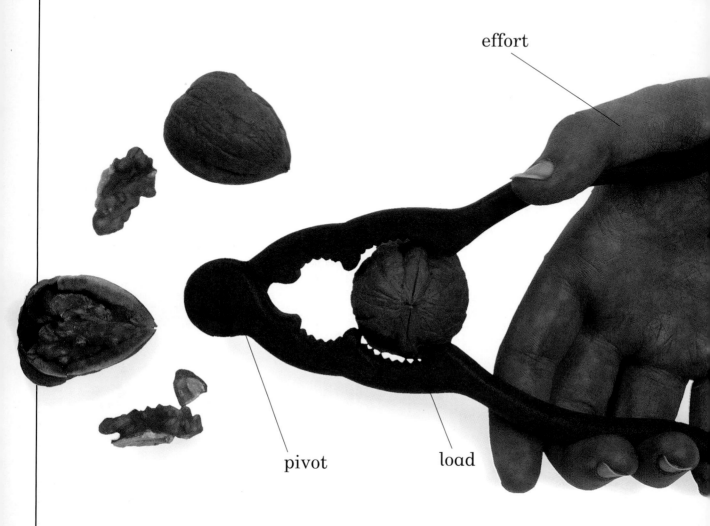

effort

pivot

load

Nutcrackers are a pair of levers with a **pivot** at one end. You can prove that they **magnify** your strength. First, try cracking a hard nut between your fingers. Unless you are superman you will not be able to. Now use the nutcrackers – it will make a big difference!

The long handles on these cutters magnify the **effort** from your arms. They can snip through thick branches. With cutters like this you can even cut through metal bars.

FACT

Cracking chimps!

Chimpanzees can crack nuts with stones. But the human being is the only animal to use levers.

FILE

Balances

This toy balance is a lever, just like a see-saw. You can experiment to see how far from the **pivot** you have to put different weights in order to make them balance.

Can you balance two weights on one side with one weight on the other side? The weight on its own must be twice as far from the pivot to make it work.

These kitchen scales use a lever to find when the weights are balanced. If you want to weigh some apples you put the apples in one pan. Next you add the weights to the other pan. If the apples weigh more than the weights, their pan stays down. If the weights weigh more, the apples go up. If the weights are equal, the pans are exactly balanced.

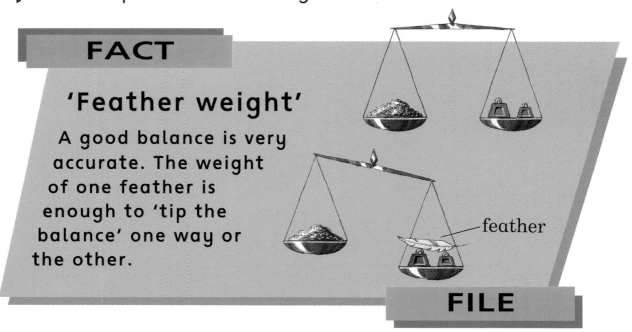

FACT

'Feather weight'

A good balance is very accurate. The weight of one feather is enough to 'tip the balance' one way or the other.

feather

FILE

Bridges

This bridge has to be lifted out of the way to let a boat pass by. It is fixed to a lever. When one end of the lever arm is pulled down, the other end pulls the bridge up into the air.

There is a heavy weight on one end of the lever arm. This weight balances most of the weight of the bridge. A person can lift the bridge with just a little extra **effort**.

Tower Bridge in London is a lever bridge. Its decks weigh about 1000 tonnes. They are balanced by huge weights. When a ship needs to pass under the bridge, electric **motors** lift up the decks.

Rods and oars

An **angler** uses levers because a fishing rod is a lever. He uses one hand as **pivot** and the other one for the **effort**. Small movements of his hands are **magnified** by the long rod. When the angler gets a bite he can move his rod very quickly.

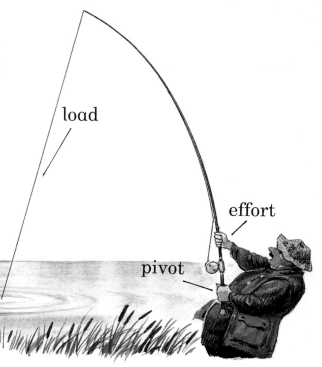

load

effort

pivot

The oars on a
rowing boat are
levers too. You
pull on the oars
to lever the
boat through
the water. The
oars pivot in
the **rowlocks**.

effort

rowlock
(pivot)

load

Brakes

brake lever

Could you stop a heavy cart like this with one hand? The answer is yes, if you use a brake lever. The lever pushes a wooden block on to the wheel. **Friction** slows the wheel down. Friction is the force that stops things from sliding easily.

Smoking brakes

Friction can make brakes so hot that they smoke or even catch fire!

The brake levers on a bicycle pull on wires. The wires pull on levers that are fixed to the frame near the wheels. These levers push rubber brake blocks onto the wheel to slow down the bicycle.

Signals

An old-fashioned railway signal was worked by levers. A person moved levers in the signal box to change the signals.

The levers pulled metal rods and made the signals change. The metal rod moved the signal arm up and down on its **pivot**.

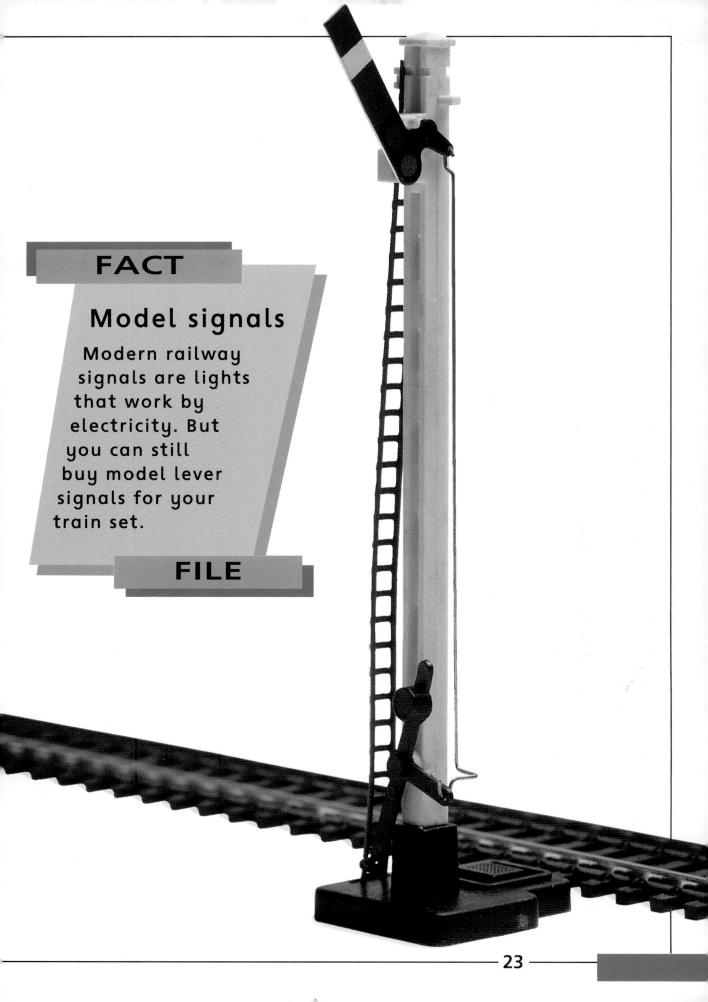

Glossary

angler   Someone who uses a rod and line to catch fish.

claw hammer   A hammer with two claws on the back of the head.

effort   The push or pull you use to move something.

friction   The drag or force that stops one thing sliding over another smoothly.

load   Something, usually heavy, that you are trying to move.

magnified   Made bigger.

motor   A machine that uses electricity or fuels such as petrol or coal to make things move.

pivot   The place around which a lever turns.

pliers   Gripping tools with jaws which you can close by squeezing a pair of handles.

rowlocks   The grips on the sides of a boat which hold the oars in place as you row.

Index

balance   4, 14, 15, 16, 17
bicycle   21
bottle opener   7
brakes   20, 21
bridges   16, 17

claw hammer   10

fishing rod   18

jaws   11

nut crackers   12

oars   18, 19

pivot   4, 5, 6, 7
pliers   11

railway signals   22, 23

see-saw   4, 14

teeth   11

wheelbarrow   8